Surviving Childhood Abuse

Living with DID (dissociative identity disorder)

Volume 1

by

Grace Carrie

www.survivingchildhoodabuse.com

1

Contents

Editor's Note

When I received this manuscript it contained a combination of writing styles. Some sections were clear, well written and articulate, but others were unclear with grammar errors and incomplete thoughts. The author said that she didn't remember writing some parts, was triggered by others, and found some parts easy to write. Given the subject matter of the book, and the authors history, we believe that some parts were written by the author, and others were written by her alters. In editing my goal was to clarify and sometimes organize, but to preserve the various writing styles. Though it was not my intent, I am sure that I also introduced my own style to the mix.

Before I met the author, I had known of no one that had DID. I am one of a few people with whom the author has shared this part of her life. She tells me that there are about 20 alters that she knows by name, and others that she is aware of, but does not know their names. I believe I have met five alters, and am aware of two more, in addition to the host personality. Two are child alters who do talk and act very much like children. I can tell when they are "out" by body language and by their distinct voices. The adult alters are harder to tell from the host which is necessary to keep their existence a secret. Sometimes they refer to the author in the third person. If I ask, they will also tell me that they are

6

not the host.

I am not educated in medicine, psychology, or psychiatry, but I am aware that there are some who would discredit the idea of DID. My thoughts are that if it helps someone to understand their world and how to deal with it, then belief in DID cannot be a bad thing. As I understand it, helping other people understand is the reason for writing this book.

The thought has crossed my mind that this could be some sort of an elaborate hoax, but after spending as much time as I have with the author, I *believe* that she is reporting her life as she experiences it. I have also not found any way that she benefits by it. If it is a hoax, it is a very elaborate one.

Disclaimer

This book is designed to provide

information on DID. This information is

provided the publisher and author do

not offer any legal or other professional

advice. In the case of a need for any such

expertise, consult with the appropriate

professional. This book does not contain

all information available on the subject.

This book has not been created to be

specific to any individual. Every effort

has been made to make this book as

accurate as possible. However, there may be errors. Therefore, this book should serve only as a general guide and not as the ultimate source of subject information. The author and publisher shall have no liability or responsibility to any person or entity regarding any loss or damage incurred, or alleged to have incurred, directly or indirectly, by the information contained in this book.

<u>*Introduction*</u>

I have known that I have multiple

personalities for a long time now. The

problem is that I live in a place where

most people think that this disorder

does not exist. Through a lot of

searching and talking to others who have

been diagnosed with this disorder, I have

learned how to manage everyday life.

Multiple personality (also known as

MPD) is now called DID. DID stands for

dissociative identity disorder. Many so-called specialists say that this disorder does not exist. I am not sure why they have come to this conclusion, but my guess would be that they cannot explain it, therefore it does not exist. However, the purpose of this book is not to argue if it exists or not. I am saying that I have it so I obviously think that it is real. What I want to accomplish with this book is to help people. I am no expert but I have dealt with this for a long time. Along the way, I have found ways to manage every day. Not everything that I suggest may work for you, but maybe it will give you some ideas. Everybody's system is different so the same thing will not work for everyone.

If you are someone who is trying to support someone with DID, I think you will find this book helpful as well. At the very least, you will be able to gain more information about this disorder. You will also learn some ways that you can help your loved one.

I am writing this book as a Q & A (question and answer). Many questions are out there about this disorder and there just is not a lot of information out there. What information you do find is often written by someone who has studied the subject. There is very little information out there that is written by someone who actually has this disorder. I think that this disorder is more common than what we know about. I believe that most people who have DID are too afraid to tell. They are probably afraid to tell because they are afraid of being labeled as "crazy". Well let me assure you that you are not crazy. The fact is that if you do have multiple personalities, you had to have gone through some really traumatic stuff in your lifetime. The fact that you are still able to get up and move around is amazing. In addition, the fact that you are reading this book means that you are trying to find out as much about this as possible, and that you are trying to learn how to move forward with your life. If

15

you hold on and stay strong things will get better. I hope that you find at least some of the information in this book helpful. You can reach me through my website (www.survivingchildhoodabuse.com) if you have any other questions that I might be able to answer.

Terms and Definitions

There is many terms that you will hear used when it comes to DID. I am just going to list a few so you will be familiar with them.

Alter – this is the term that some people use when they are referring to one of the different personalities

Being out – this often the term used when the host or another personality is out

Big or older – this is referring to adult
alters

Co-present – this is when two
personalities are out at the same time

Front – this is referring to the foremost
part of your mind or awareness. When
an alter is out we say they are up front.
When one is close to the front, they are
aware of what is happening but not in
complete control.

Integration – this I when all personalities
merge into one. I do not agree with this.

Little – this term is what we use for child
alters

Lost time – time not remembered when
another alter is out

Singleton – someone who does not have

DID

Multiple – someone who does have DID

Splitting / switching – when another alter comes out

Host – main personality

System – term used to describe how all alters work together

What is DID/multiple personalities?

Dissociative identity disorder

(DID) is the same thing as multiple

personality disorder. You will see it being

called DID more often that multiple

personality these days. It is an illness

that is characterized by the presence of

at least two clear personality states, also

called alters, which may have different

reactions, emotions, thoughts, and even

body functioning.

What is dissociation?

It is a defense mechanism where

we separate out of memory things that

we do not want to, or cannot, handle.

Everyone dissociates at some point.

Have you ever been driving home and,

once you got there, you cannot really remember the details of your drive? This is a form of dissociation. When trauma is happening dissociation can be useful. When dissociation becomes a primary defense mechanism, it can become full-blown DID, which is when alters are created. People can still use dissociation even when alters are not created. Dissociation is when we block certain details from our everyday awareness.

When childhood is difficult or abusive, dissociation can become a primary defense mechanism, because children can easily get overwhelmed and "check out", or dissociate, when they cannot handle what is going on. If you don't learn other coping skills then you may continue to use dissociation, even in your adult life. You may not even notice that you are dissociating. It becomes automatic. The problem is that dissociation can become too automatic and happen at times when you do not really need it. Then it becomes a

negative coping skill because it leaves

you out of touch with reality and

unaware of what is going on around you.

If you find that you are dissociating

without the presence of alters you can

try to make a point to be more aware of

what is going on around you. Replay the

situation over in your head and make a

conscious effort not to forget it.

What causes DID?

The specific cause of DID is still

23

unknown but it seems to all be tied to these possible causes:

- Severe physical, mental, and sexual abuse in childhood
- lack of a supportive or comforting person to counteract the abuse

The primary cause of DID appears to be severe and prolonged trauma that occurs during childhood. It can be emotional, physical or sexual abuse. Young children, who are subjected to torture, sexual abuse or neglect,

dissociate by creating separate identities

or personalities (or alters) because the

abuse they are facing is more than they

can handle. An alter may suffer while the

primary identity (host) is "protected"

from the unbearable experience.

Dissociation is easy for a child to achieve

and it becomes a useful and needed

defense. Over time the child may create

more alters, as different situations arise.

I have about 25 alters that I have names

for, and I am aware of others. Often an

alter may be created to handle one specific job or even to be a companion for the child during a very hard and lonely time.

A sad fact is that child abuse does occur. Studies have shown that if a child is abused and hey have an adult who helps them work through the effects of abuse that they suffer less long term effects than a child who does not have a supportive person in their life.

How common is DID?

It is said that only about 9% of people have DID. I believe that the number is higher. Most people with DID are not quick to say that they have it. Often people who are being seen by a mental health professional are diagnosed with something other than DID when, in fact, they have DID. I think people are misdiagnosed because there are many people in the mental health field who still refuse to acknowledge that this is a real disorder.

What are the symptoms of DID?

For each person who has DID, the symptoms can be different, but we will talk about some common ones here.

- **Mood swings** – this is because each alter usually has their own personality. People who do not know that we have DID might just think that we are moody. I know that this is often the case for me. In reality, though, I am very stable with my moods when there are no alters out.

- **Suicidal tendencies or self-harm** - I have had times in the past where I just wanted to die to end all the pain. If you find yourself in this place, please reach out for help and support anywhere you can. I promise once you have learned how everything inside you works , you will be able to lead a fulfilling life.

  Self-harm is often listed with suicide, although, I do not agree that it should be. Self-harm can be many different forms. It can be

cutting, burning, hitting and many

other things that people do to

themselves BUT IT IS NOT A

SUICIDE ATTEMPT. Often people

who self-harm hurt so much on

the inside that they need

something on the outside to show

that pain. It also can be a

controlling attempt, if they are

going to hurt anyway then at least

they get to control it. It also can

simply be a cry for help. I know for

me it was a little of all of those. I

cut for many years until I realized

that this coping mechanism no

longer worked. I was not able to

stop cutting overnight. It took me

a long time to learn other ways of

dealing with things and there are

still times when I want to cut, but I

just remind myself that it does not

solve anything it only numbs it for

a while. Although I have quit self-

harming I have alters who still do

this. With the help of a friend,

who gives me a lot of support, I have managed to calm some of my alters down so they do not self-harm as often, but it still happens at times. I think the key to getting the alters to stop is helping them to realize that it no longer works or that it is no longer needed. Sometimes I find that an alter cuts me when they get angry or upset. Try talking to them, if possible, and see if you can get them to talk about why they are angry instead of cutting. If you

have a friend that the alter will

talk to, then maybe your friend

can calm them down. If this does

not work and an alter ends up

self-harming, remember that this

habit cannot be changed

overnight and keep trying until

you find something that works.

- **Sleep disorders (insomnia, night

   terrors)**- Insomnia is a chronic lack of

   sleep. It can be caused by many

things. Many times for me it is caused by a little alter who is too scared to sleep. I have to constantly try to find ways to calm them down so that we can all get some sleep. It is a constant battle because when I find something that works, it works for a while, but then stops working. The best advice I can offer here is to try to calm them any way you can. Offer them a blanket or stuffed animal to sleep with. My little alters like to talk to my friend, who they look at as their mother, and they have a blanket. This often calms them down so that they can go to sleep. Unfortunately, the problem does not just end when they go to sleep. Once asleep, there is always the possibility of night terrors. Night terrors are sleep disturbances in which a person may suddenly sit straight up in bed, cry, scream, moan, mumble and toss about with their eyes wide open, but without being truly awake. Night terrors are more frightening and realistic than an ordinary nightmare. When I wake

from a night terror, it often sends me

into a violent round of flashbacks. It is

hard for me to distinguish my past

from my present. If I am the one who

is out when I wake up, I try to ground

myself to the present. I get up and

walk around, look at present pictures,

say aloud what is around me, feel my

feet on the floor, anything that

reminds me of where I am. The

bigger problem for me is when one of

my little alters is out when I wake up

36

from a night terror. This never turns
out well. Many times an older alter
will come out and think that we are in
danger again and try to protect us as
she sees fit. On the other hand, if the
little alter remains out she gets up
and roams around and none of us
gets any sleep that night. Sometimes
my little alters will try to talk to my
friend, which helps, but it doesn't
happen often enough. If you find this
happening to you, find things that
make you or your alters calm. Try to

calm down and maybe you will be able to go back to sleep. If one thing doesn't work, don't be afraid to try something else. If holding a blanket or bear helps you feel calmer so you can sleep, then by all means do that. Sleep is important! Your days will be much easier if you get enough rest the night before. So it doesn't matter how silly it seems. If it works do it.

- **Anxiety, panic attacks, and phobias (flashbacks, reactions to stimuli or**

"triggers") - Learn what your triggers are. There are several reasons why you need to learn them. Often an alter will come out when something happens that is triggering. By learning what your triggers are, you may find ways to avoid them all together or be able to work on handling them better. I still have not learned what all my triggers are, but I know some of them. I have been able to manage some of them better over time, but I have not been able to learn to manage others, so I do my best to

avoid them. Anxiety and panic attacks

are very real and at times can make

you feel like you cannot breathe or

are having a heart attack. If this

happens a lot, please see a doctor.

Living with DID has enough problems

that cannot be solved by a doctor.

There is no point in suffering from

something when a doctor can help.

- **Alcohol and drug abuse** – Although I

  have not had this problem, I do know

that some people do. From what I
can tell, this is just another way to
deal with the pain from the past.
Avoiding the problem does not solve
it. You have to work through the pain
and issues. If you are dealing with this
problem, I urge you to find help.
There are many places that offer
help. You must find healthier ways to
deal with the pain.

- **Loss of time** – Lost time happens

  because an alter is out, you usually

41

do not remember anything that
happens while they are out. I will talk
later in this book about how to
manage lost time.

- **Frequent Headaches** – No one has
been able to tell me why headaches
occur with DID. I do know that when
strong alters come out my head often
hurts afterwards. I will also get a
headache if I am trying to stop an
alter from coming out. Other times I
get headaches when my head is too

loud. It makes sense to me that

people with DID get headaches all the

time because their brain is constantly

working. My suggestion is to treat

this just like a normal headache. If

you normally take something for

headaches then do so. If taking

medication does not work then try

lying down. For me I usually just have

to wait it out until it goes away.

- **Feeling like watching a movie rather than living own life** – This one is hard to explain, but if you have ever

experienced it, you will know what it

is like. Sometimes when I think back

on my past it is as if I am watching a

movie.I feel detatched from it as

though it is someone else's life.

Sometimes I even feel like that when

I think back on what I have done

during the day,. Often when I feel this

way people around me will tell me

that I seemed very distant that day. I

think that this happens on days when

I split a lot, or days when some of my

44

alters are really close to the surface. I feel like I am walking around in a daze when this happens. Almost like life is not real.

- **Hearing voices** – My head can be very loud at times. I can hear some of my alters just as if I were talking to someone in real life. When I am having a particularly stressful day, I can sometimes hear all of them talking at once. I cannot always make out what they are saying, but I can hear them. Sometimes I will hear my child alters crying and I will have to go make sure that it is not one of *my* children crying. Hearing voices can be confusing at times, but as you learn how your system works and get to know your alters better, things will quiet down some. At least they have for me.

What are coping mechanisms?

Coping mechanisms can also be

referred to as survival skills or defense mechanisms. They are strategies that we use to deal with situations that stress us. Everyone learns coping mechanisms in different ways and at different times. For those of us who have been abused it is likely that some of our coping mechanisms are learned during the time of our abuse. Some are good and some are bad. Some bad examples would be drinking, drugs, eating disorders and self-harm. Some good examples would be relaxation, exercise, calling a friend and writing in a journal. Whether they are good or bad we use them to benefit us in some way. We experience many different situations in life and we have responses to those situations. There are mental, emotional, physical, and behavioral responses. By learning to recognize our emotions, we are better able to determine if our coping mechanisms are still doing us any good. If you find that a coping mechanism is doing more harm than good then you can take steps to learn different cooping skills that have a more positive effect. If you find yourself coping with things in a negative way, try to find different ways to handle stress that have a more positive effect. This will not happen overnight, it will take a lot of hard work and time. Do not be hard on yourself when trying to change negative coping mechanisms. At one point, these coping mechanisms did work for you, and they got you through some very difficult times.

What is a system?

Everyone who has DID has a "system". This simple mean that all the alters and host have a way of working together. They all have their jobs. No two people's systems are alike but they all usually have a basic structure. It may look something like this.

- **The main one** - this personality is usually very strong and has an influence on all the others (like a boss)

- **The adults** – do what normal

adults do like watching the kids, cooking, cleaning, working , shopping, driving, handling stressful situations

- **The kids** –much like real children they like to color or play. They often hold many memories from the past so they may have a lot of hurt, pain and anger.

- **Self-destructive** – these can cause many problems if not watched. They often hold a lot of anger towards the host. They might think that the host could have stopped the abuse or gotten away. They might think that the host still cannot do anything right. They are often out during periods of self-mutilation or suicide attempts. Now here is where I would like to clear a few things up: You might read in other places that these alters will try to kill the host, but I believe that this is not true. I believe that they can be the ones who attempt suicide, but I believe that they do it to end their own pain. Their purpose is not to kill you. After all, the reason why alters were created is so that we could live through something that we ordinarily would not be able to live through. It was the alters job to try to ensure that we lived, so why would they want to kill us now?

Do people with DID commonly let other

people know that they have it?

I would say no, not usually. The few people that I know of who have DID are not willing to let many people know. I know I don't. They are very good at hiding it. They will not tell anyone until they are absolutely sure that person is "safe". They often feel like no one can be trusted. This is because they were hurt as a child and they learned this very early on. Most of these people have known a lot of fear, denial, betrayal, and pain. They have learned that keeping

things a secret is important to survival.

Have you always known that you had

DID?

No, I didn't always know I had DID

and I do not think anyone does. A child

who is experiencing the kind of abuse

that I did is not thinking about how they

are surviving it. They are just trying to

live day to day. I always knew that I

heard voices and that I did not

remember certain things. I just thought

55

this was normal. I thought everyone was like that. It was not until I was in my late teens that I finally figured out what was going on. As I got older, I realized that the voices I was hearing did not sound like my own. The voices did not think as I did either. I also began to see that things were being done, apparently by me, but I had no memory of doing them. I would find work that I had signed but it was not my name. I then started to pay close attention to just how much time I was losing and was surprised to learn just how much I was missing. I also came

to realize that while I did remember

being abused , I did not remember all of

it. I also realized that the imaginary

friends I had as a child were still with

me. (I would soon learn that it was my

child alters that I had been hearing all

this time) At the time I was reading a

book and it mentioned something about

DID. In the book was a testimonial of a

woman who said she had DID. It was

almost as if I was reading about me. One

day I just decided to ask the voices in my

head what was going on. I wrote in a journal and one of them responded back to me. I simply wrote, "Could someone please tell me what is going on". The reply I got was "hi it's nice to finally get to talk to you. I am one of many here who have helped you over the years. I am the one that the others look to as the main one. Please do not be scared. We are not here to hurt you. I am sure all this is confusing but we will get through this too". I was shocked when I read this and I was scared, even though she had said not to be. Then I realized that they

had always been there and nothing had

changed by me realizing that they were.

Once I accepted it, I was relieved. Then I

understood why I was the way I was.

What does it feel like to have DID?

For me it is like having a whole

world inside me; a whole community. I

am never alone, although sometimes I

wish I were. Whenever things get

stressful, I switch and someone else

takes over. If I am too tired or in too

much pain someone else will come out

who does not get tired or does not feel

pain . For this reason, some people think

that DID is an awesome coping

mechanism, which it is. It has allowed

me to live through the some horrible

things, but it does get frustrating at

times. For example, I have missed many

things that my kids have done through

the years because I was not the one who

was out at the time. I also have very few

friends because I am too afraid that they

will find out that I have DID and that I

60

will somehow get hurt when they do. I
have spent a lot of my life feeling
alienated from the world due, in part, to
the fact that I have DID. Having DID can
cause you to feel very lonely even with
so many others inside you. For years, I
did not let anyone get close to me.
Recently, I met someone who has
become a dear friend. I was lucky
because she accepts me for who I am
and accepts my alters as well.

What are triggers?

Triggers are things that bring out alters, flashbacks, thoughts, feelings (these can even be physical). Some things you might find triggering are smells, places, actions, sensations, body language, certain phrases or words. It can be many different things. You might not ever learn what all your triggers are, but over time, you will learn what some of them are. As you do, you will learn to either avoid them or to manage your reaction to them.

How to handle times when you are triggered?

Now that we have talked about what triggers are, let us talk about how to handle them. You first have to know what your triggers are. This can be the hardest part because a trigger can be anything, big or small. It can be a word, a smell, or even the way that someone walks.   My suggestion, when you are trying to figure out what triggers you, is to keep a journal. If you notice that you have been triggered, jot down what happened right before. Eventually you will be able to see patterns that will help you discover what is triggering you. Once you learn what triggers you, you can start anticipating them and prepare for them so you can manage them better. I find that, if I am ready for a trigger it does not seem to be as bad as it would be if I was caught off guard. When you find that you are triggered, try doing something physical. Look around and remind yourself of where you are; do something that takes a lot of mental concentrtion; or talk it out with someone you trust. I know that my therapist taught me many good ways to handle triggers that worked for me. If you find yourself having a really hard time with triggers then you might consider finding yourself a good therapist.

It is all in your head; can you not just make it stop?

Oh, this question used to make me

see red. I so badly want to say, "Well of course it is in my head". After all that is where my brain is and that is where DID originates. So in a way, yes it is in my head, but definitely not in the way that the people who are asking this question are thinking. No, you cannot just make it stop. It is real and there is nothing you can do to change that. You might be able to ignore it for a while, but I have found that only makes things worse. Try not to let questions like this get you upset. The people that ask these questions do so because they truly do not know or

understand DID.

Are alters really real?

I have heard this question a lot and

honestly, I do not know exactly what it

means, but my answer is yes. My alters

all have their own feelings and ideas.

Some are left-handed and some are right

handed. Some like fish some do not.

Some need my glasses some do not. One

likes hotdogs which I can't stand. They

are all different so to me they are very

real.

How and when do separate alters show themselves?

Often times alters show

themselves when the job that they do is

needed or when something triggers

them. In my system I have different

alters who have different jobs. I have

some who handle and talk to certain

people in my life. I have some who talk

to people when we are in public. I also
have some that handle stress. I have
some who are strong and angry who
come out when they think we are in
danger. I also have child alters that come
out at odd times. Sometimes an alter will
come out just because they want to.
Having alters come out unexpectedly
can make life really hard at times.

Is only one personality out at a time?

There are times when my alters
are really close to the surface. At these

times, it is as if they are partially out at the same time that I am. I know this is happening because the alter will be aware of what is going on around me and have opinions about the situation. I can hear their opinions. At times, I believe they are the ones talking to people around me and I am still able to hear it. I know this because they are saying things that I normally would say.

Should you try to integrate your alters?

You might have heard talk about integrating. This basically means that a therapist would try to help combine all the personalities in to one. I absolutely do not like this idea at all. I think the best solution is to get all your alters to work together. I also think it is important to show your alters that you are no longer "stuck in your abuse" and that you are stronger than you used to be. It is also important to remember that your alters were hurt too. They have thoughts and feelings that need to be healed.

Once they begin to heal and see that you are healing too, and stronger than you used to be, maybe they will see that you do not need to be protected as much as you did in the past. Then you can work on trying to get everyone to work together. This will help to reduce the number of times that you split in a day. This can take a while to accomplish. I still have times where I do not remember most of my day. Please be patient with your alters because they are only doing what they were created to do.

Remember you have alters because at one point you could not do it own your own. It will take time for your alters to believe that you are safe and that they are safe as well.

Are different personalities aware of each other?

This is not a simple question. I do believe that most of my alters are aware of each other although they may not communicate with the each other. I am

73

not completely sure of how many alters that I have so there is a possibility that I do have some that are not aware of the others. If this were the case then I would desperately want to reach out to them because I know that they are living a very lonely life. Especially if they are not aware of the fact that we are no longer in the abusive situation that we once were in.

Is it true that people who have DID are usually very intelligent?

Yes, in most cases, this is true, but you will never get us to admit it. The reason we do not admit it is that we know that, if it were not for the alters, we would not be able to do half the things that we can. I have alters that are good at remembering everything. I have some that are good at fixing things. I have some that are good in school subjects. I have some that are good at writing. When I need the answer to a question, or I need to know how to do something, I just ask whoever is good at that particular thing. I read very fast but never remember what I read until I need it. This is because I am usually not the one who reads it. When I was in college, I would read the chapter and when I went to take the test, I all of a sudden would be able to see the words in front of me, so I could answer the questions correctly. This is because one of my alters read it and was able to bring it to my memory when I needed it. You could say that I have a photographic memory.

So for me to say that I am intelligent

would just not be right, but I will say that

together, my alters and I, are able to do

most things. I sometimes wonder if high

intelligence is necessary for a person to

split when they are experiencing

something they can't handle, or whether

having alters makes us, as a group, more

intelligent, because we draw on the skills

of each alter. I don't know the answer

to this question.

Why don't other people realize that you have switched?

This is not very hard to understand. Everyone knows someone who would be considered "moody". That is why people do not notice. They probably just think I am moody, and at times unstable. Now the friends, who know that I have DID, says that it is obvious when I split. They say that I move my eyes back and forth when I split and that when I come back I always

look around me as if I am "seeing where

I am at". They only notice this because

they already know that I sometimes

split. Most people think I am a dreamer

and that I am just dazed sometimes. I

like it this way. I do not want many

people knowing about my having DID.

What is a typical day like when you have DID?

I would like to be able to say that a

typical day with DID is not much

different from a day without it but that just would not be true. I will say that if you have DID, you will have good and bad days just like someone without DID.

So let us start with the GOOD DAYS. Good days would not be that much different from most people. I work and take care of my kids. I keep the house clean and clothes done. I enjoy walks outside and going to the mall. On good days, I remember about 80-90% of my day. The only difference is that I might have alters doing these things with me. I might have a child alter come out to color a picture, pet the animals,ride the escalator at the mall,or even have an ice cream. I have a close friend who my child alters look to as a mom. They love to come out and spend time with her. She gives them things that any child would like. On a good day, I might also have an older alter come out who just wants to take a walk or sit an enjoy a book. To me all of this is very normal and is easy to handle.

Now for the bad days. These are the days when I cannot find my glasses because an alter who doesn't need them has been out all morning and has left them somewhere, unknown to me. Or I go to the grocery store and come out only to realize that I do not know where the car is because it was an alter who parked it. Or the days when I have to check my bank to make sure I have money because one of my alters might have figured out the pin to my card and used it without me knowing. Or I come back out in the middle of a conversation and have to figure out what we are talking about. I often wonder if I have fed the kids or given them a bath. And all of this is just minor stuff.

There are days when I lose hours at a time with no idea of what I have been doing. There have been times where I lose whole days and that is really confusing. There are days when I come out and realize that my best friend and I are arguing and I do not know why.

Often the reason is that an alter has come out and said some very mean things, that I would never say, and my friend did not know that it was not me. Some mornings I wake up to find that an alter has self-harmed. On my bad days, I just want to go to bed but when bedtime finally comes, I sometimes can't even do that because of a crying child alter. They might be crying because they are scared, or because they did not get "their" time to come out and play that day. And if by some chance, the child alter ends up

84

going to sleep, it may not last long,

because they often wake up with

nightmares. Or if I fall to sleep, I may

wake up with nightmares. All of this only

just begins to describe what a bad day is

like. If I am lucky I have more good days

than bad, but I am not always lucky.

Sometimes my bad days outnumber the

good ones. Because the bad days take so

much energy, it often takes me awhile to

recover from them.

If you find yourself having a bad

day that really takes a lot out of you,

please be easy on to yourself. If it is the

middle of the day and you feel like you

could lie down and take a nap, then lie

down and take a nap. It may be the only

chance you get to rest that day. Take a

bath and read a book if you enjoy those

things. Try not to push yourself to hard.

How to handle angry alters?

Handling angry alters can be tough

at times. There are many different

reasons why an alter might be angry.

They could be angry because they think

that you should have been able to stop,

or get away from, the abuse. Maybe

they think that you somehow made a

bad decision that got you abused.

Maybe they are angry with you for

creating them and causing them to have

to live through the abuse as well. Maybe

they are angry about an everyday

situation, like you and I might be, but

they may seem overly angry because in

the past they had to appear to be strong

and unshakable. Being angry is often just a front. Depending on why the alter is angry, calming the alter down may take some time.

I would suggest trying to let them get their anger out either by to talking to you, by getting them to write in a journal, or by talking to a trusted friend. When trying to talk to them, make sure that you always come across as calm and try not to argue, which will only make them angrier. If they will not talk to you,

see if they will write about why they are

angry in a journal or notebook. Then you

can reply to them the same way. . If you

have someone you trust that you talk to,

maybe the alter would talk to them as

well. Sometimes it helps to have an

outside point of view.

However you communicate with them,

try to get them to see that they were not

the only one that was hurt, and that if

you could have changed anything you

would have in a heartbeat. They first

have to realize that *you* were not able to

control any of it. Try to be very

understanding when you are talking to

them. Remember they were hurt too.

Let them know how much you

appreciate all the help that they gave

you. Let them know that it is OK that

they are angry and it is OK to express

that anger. Think about how you would

want to be talked to by someone if it

were you who was angry. You may find

that you learn a lot just by hearing their

stories.

Also, finding healthy ways for an alter to "vent" when they are angry is a great idea. Let them go for a walk, tear up paper, workout, do anything that helps them get the anger out in a nondestructive way. Anger in its self is not a bad thing. It is what is done with that anger that can be bad.

What can you do when one alter becomes angry with another alter?

To me this is the worst-case scenario, and can totally disrupt the whole system. Think about an army for a minute. This army is working together to win a war, right? Well now, think about what happens if a war breaks out INSIDE the army. What would happen then? Everyone would lose, right? Well that is what happens when you have alters that fight each other. Everyone loses. You lose because often your head will become so loud that you cannot focus on anything. You also lose because you may start to feel the feelings that the

alter feels, and not be aware of where

the feelings are coming from. The alters

lose because they will be in total chaos

all the time. In particular, the child alters

lose if they become afraid of the older

alters; and they do not need any more

fear than they already have. Everyone

loses and it is possible that you could

end up losing the battle that we call life.

It is important to try to keep your system

working together as much as possible.

If you have tried everything you can to calm an alter down and it is not working, then it might be time to ask for help. Ask everyone inside your system if there is an alter that is stronger than the one that is angry. If there is then ask the stronger one to carry the angry alter towards the back somewhere until they have calmed down. When you ask for help remember to mindful and listen carefully. Some of the other ones might very well know what is bothering the angry alter and might have suggestions that will help.

How to handle lost time?

First, you have to see that there really is no lost time. The time is there you just might not be *out* to experience, and remember it. I have found that keeping a journal helps a lot. I have used a small notebook that I kept in my pocket or even on your phone. I ask everyone who comes out to jot down what they do so, when I come back out, I know what happened. You can also ask one alter to be in charge of updating you when you come out. Another way to handle lost time is to work on internal communication. Come up with a plan. Plan times when certain alters can come out. Give the child alters their time out to play. This way you know that everything that you need to accomplish that day will be done and the alters will have their time out as well. And you do not have to be as worried about what they do while they are out.

Tips and advise (for what it's worth).

Living with DID can be challenging

at times to say the least. It took me

years to figure out what worked for me. I

would like to share a few tips with you.

They might not work for you but they

might give you some ideas.

As I mentioned earlier lost time is

the biggest issue. I have really found that keeping a journal helps the most.

Keeping a journal allows everyone to have a chance to talk. They can write whatever they want to. The little ones can draw pictures if they want to. This will help them feel like they are being heard and will allow you to know what is going on with everyone.

Another thing that I have found that helps is to keep everything around you organized and try not to move

things very often. As long I as keep
things organized then all my alters know
where everything is and things that need
to be done, usually are done.

A long time ago, I always seemed
to have less money than I thought I
should. I soon realized that my alters
where spending money when they were
out. I started changing the code to my
debit card at least twice a month and
now I keep some money in a lock box
that is locked with a code. I also keep

some money in my pocket so that whoever is out will have a little bit of cash if they need it. This does not always work but it does help. I also make sure that I pay my bills as soon as I have the money, so at least I know that they are paid.

If I find myself switching a lot and I need to stay present then I find that doing something physical or something that takes a lot of concentration helps to slow the switching down. If that does not work then I try talking to whoever wants out and ask if they can wait until later. Once again, sometimes this works and sometimes it does not. If I have an alter who has been triggered to come out because they sense danger there usually is nothing I can do to stop it. I have just learned to trust my alters. After all, they have gotten me through a lot worse situations than anything that happens to me today.

Personal Experience

While writing this book I experienced a mayor crisis, as I would call it. I have debated whether to write about it or not because I do not want to scare anyone, but although it was hard, I did learn a lot from it, and it is reality. I think it is important to realize how important communication really is and that there is always learning to be done .

I think that this situation sums it all up

very well.

I have a couple who are my closest

friends. For the purpose of this story we

will call them James and Margaret. I

have known Margaret for a little over

two years and have known her husband,

James, for about a year. Margaret is the

first person I have ever told about my

DID. She has accepted me and all of my

alters without question. Her husband

also knows and has accepted it. They
have helped my kids and me so much.
We actually live with them right now.
Margaret has another friend who also
has a rough past. Margaret is also
supporting her other friend in her
healing journey. Margaret has a really
big heart and wants to help everyone.
Margaret's other friend is really jealous
of me and that has been a problem for
well over a year now. Margaret's answer
to keep her other friend from being hurt
was just to keep me and her other friend

completely separate. Even to the point that when she talks to her other friend I am never mentioned, as if I do not even exist. This really hurts me because I have always felt like I have not been seen or heard. Although Margaret never treats me like that it still hurt that she had that part of her where she acted as if I was not around. I tried several times to explain it to her, but I never succeeded in getting her to understand what was going on. She believed that I was jealous, like her other friend, and that I didn't have any reason to be. Every time I tried

to talk to her about it, and explain that it

had nothing to do with jealousy, I sensed

a resistance and that she was not ready

to hear what I had to say, so I backed

down and just ignored the problem. The

truth was that for a long time I have felt

like she always choose her other friend

over me, as if I was second to her. I was

OK with this even though it did hurt. I

told myself that I loved her too much as

a friend, and did not want to lose her, so

I would just live with that hurt and not

bring it up again. After all, in my mind, I had been hurt a lot worse. The problem is that even if I choose to overlook when I am hurt, my alters do not always think that is best. After all, it is there job to try to keep me from being hurt.

On this weekend, Margaret had gone away for the weekend to visit her other friend because her other friend did not want to come to Margaret's house because I am here. Everything came to a head and the problem could no longer be ignored. Jessica, one of my stronger alters, who has also tried to help my friend see that I was being hurt, had had enough. She came out and refused to allow the problem to be ignored any longer. She tried again to explain things to Margaret. Because this has been an issue for so long, Margaret got defensive and still would not listen to what Jessica was trying to tell her. It never was Margaret's intention to hurt me in any way, and she just could not understand why I was being hurt. When she couldn't get through to Margaret, Jessica decided that Margaret's house was no longer

that best place for my kids and me. So,

she packed what she could in a small

backpack and had intentions of leaving.

Lucky for me, James was home at that

time and quickly realized what was

about to happen. He was not able to to

keep her from leaving that day but did

get her to agree to come back that night.

She did leave and with her out, my kids

and I spent all day walking around town

and riding buses. We ended up at the

airport, which is where Jessica let me

back out. I called James, who came and picked us up. Everyone was hoping that everything would be over that night, but I knew that it was far from over. I tried my best to reason with Jessica and explain that this was the best place for us and that I did not want to leave, but she kept telling me that she had been unable to protect me in the past, but she was able to protect me now, and that she was going to do it. She too felt as if Margaret was making the choice to hurt me, and that was not going to happen anymore.

The second day Margaret was gone Jessica once again packed our bag and left with the kids. James was unable to get her to agree to come back that night probably because Jessica did not intend to let me come back. With Jessica out again my kids and I spent all day in the city, heading south from what I can tell. She obviously was trying to get out-of-town. Some of my other alters, who are not as strong as Jessica, so they could not come out to take us home, convinced Anna, who is stronger than

Jessica, to come out. Anna

communicated with James through text

message and James convinced her to

come back home. Anna agreed to come

back home but only with the promise

that we would try to find an answer that

would satisfy Jessica. Anna got us home,

as she had promised, but it was really

late and well past dark. Just to be clear,

my kids were never aware that anything

was going wrong, they just thought that I

was taking them on an adventure for

those two days, and they had a great time. My alters would never do anything to put my kids in danger and that knowledge really helped to put my mind at ease while this was all happening.

Margaret was back from her trip by the time that we arrived back at the house. We all decided that it was time for Jessica and Margaret to talk about what was going on and see if a solution could be reached. We didn't find a solution that night, but did find one over the next few days.

Everyone involved learned a lot that weekend. I learned that I should not just ignore when I am being hurt, even if it is by my best friend who is hurting me, and even if I don't think that it is a big deal. I think that Margaret learned to listen better and that she did not have to understand why something hurt me, she just needed to accept that it did. James learned how to communicate and reason with my alters, which is not always easy to do. Most importantly, I learned to listen to my alters. I found out that Jessica's job on the many nights I

was abused was to decide who was

going to be out during the abuse, me or

one of my child alters. I could not

imagine having to make that choice. I

also learned that, for the most, part my

alters think more of me than I think of

myself, and I need to learn from that. I

also learned that most of the alters do

not like their jobs. They would much

rather I learn how to handle things so

that they can come out just because

they want to, not because they have to.

As hard as that weekend was I think we all learned a lot and made a lot of progress to understanding even more about how my system works, and how important communication really is. I do not *just* mean communication between myself and my alters, but also with my friends, especially those who are aware that I have DID. I also learned a lot more about triggers. The whole time I was being hurt I just thought that it was a trigger that I needed to get over and learn to deal with better. I now realize the difference between a trigger and a hurt. A trigger is something that reminds you of a hurt from the past, but that hurt is not being repeated in the present. What my friend was doing was triggering me, reminding me of a past hurt, but was also continuing to hurt me in the present. That is something that I should not just ignore.

Mayor crises like this are very rare for me, but the reality is that they do happen, especially if problems are not properly handled when they arise. I might have been able to live with the

hurt my friend was causing, but my

alters could not. I am not mad at Jessica.

I think she made some bad choices but I

also think that she helped Margaret and

I resolve a real issue. She forced a

problem to to light and a solution to be

found, for which I am grateful.

When you are having a bad day or

even a crisis like this one. I encourage

you to find the good points about it. See

what is to be learned from it. Do not

focus so much on the fact that it

happened becaue you cannot change

the fact that it did. Instead, focus on the

good points and learn what to do

differently next time.

Note to survivors with DID:

If you have just found out that you

have DID I am sure that your mind is

racing everywhere. It can be

overwhelming but I do promise that with

some work things will get better. You

will have bad days but the good ones will

eventually outnumber the bad days.

Some of the things that you have read in

this book will probably not work for you,

but you might get a few ideas of some

things to try. Don t be afraid to talk to

your alters. They are not your enemy.

They have been with you for a long time

and their job has been to help you get to

where you are. Try to build

communication with them. Listen to

what they are telling you. If something is

120

triggering them then try your best to

figure out what is triggering them, why it

is triggering them, and to find some

common ground. Be patient in the

process of learning to communicate with

your alters. It will take some time. If you

have alters that want time out then try

to find time to let that happen. If you

have alters that are insisting that you are

in danger, and that you are about to be

hurt, listen to them. At least hear them

out. Maybe they see something that you

do not see. If there is no danger that you

can see, tell them that. It could be that they are just triggered by something and maybe you can all work together to find something that will work for them, and for you.

I encourage you to find at least one person who you can tell about DID, and who will support you along the way. That person can be a friend or family member or therapist. I think that support is vitally important to dealing with DID. Often times just having someone who will listen, when you are

having a bad day, makes all the

difference in the world. Please hang in

there. Do not give up. Reach out for help

if you need it. You can always ask me

questions at my website:

www.survivingchildhoodabuse.com

Notes to supporters

It can be frightening to watch a

loved one deal with DID. You may feel

helpless at times, but there *are* ways

that you can help.

- You can learn all you can about DID.
  The more you know and understand
  the better you will be able to help. I
  urge you to make sure that, in your
  search for information, you try to
  make sure that the information that
  you find comes from trusted sources.
  There is a lot of information out
  there, but a good bit of it is false, or
  written by someone who has never

even met a person with DID. I believe

that, if you do not have DID, or know

someone who does, then there is no

way you can know much about it.

- You can help your loved one with DID

  find a therapist if you and your loved

  one think one is needed. I do not

  think that it is necessary to see a

  therapist if DID is managed and

  everyday life is going well. I have

  never seen a therapist just because I

  have DID. Now I have seen a therapist

when my depression, anxiety, or
flashbacks became too bad. If your
loved one is having a hard time with
any of these, then I would suggest
that they see a professional. There
are different ways to treat these
including talk therapy and
medication. I do not think people
should suffer , when there are
treatments that can help them.
Sometimes when a person is stressed
or depressed, they have a hard time
just getting out of bed in the

morning. You can help by phoning

around and finding out what

therapists there are in your area. You

can also help by finding out which

ones are covered by your loved ones

insurance. If they do not have

insurance, you could check into

options for free therapy. Most states

offer free therapy to those who

qualify. If you start by calling your

local health department, they should

be able to point you in the right

direction. If you do succeed in finding

a therapist for your loved one, and they agree to go, you could offer to go with them if they would like for you too. Sometimes it helps just knowing that someone is there.

- You can just listen, without judging. You might not have any suggestions or any advice, but by listening, you are allowing them to sort out their thoughts, and that can have a huge impact. Your loved ones head might be so loud that they cannot even think straight. Having the chance to

say aloud what they are thinking can

help them get their thoughts straight,

and they may be able to discover the

answers to their problems. You do

not have to have all the answers. Just

listening might very well be the

answer they are looking for.

- You can keep in mind that your loved

  one with DID might "switch". This

  means that another alter or

  personality might come out. Other

alters might sound and act different from your loved one. They will have their own thoughts, likes, dislikes, and opinions. It is possible for an alter not to even know who you are. If you think that you are talking to an alter "just ask them". Sometimes they will tell you and sometimes they won't. Do not push them to tell you if they do not want to. Just introduce yourself, if they do not know you, and be courteous of their feelings. If they seem confused about where they are then tell them where they are and what is going on. Offer reassurance if they seem scared or anxious. If they appear to be mad, ask them what has them angry. It could be just an angry alter and that is just how they are. Watch carefully what you say to alters. You do not want to say anything that could be upsetting or offensive. Your goal should be to earn their trust. You want them to see you as "safe". Lastly, do not hold what an alter says against your loved ones, just because an alter says it does not mean that your loved one feels the same. In the beginning I am sure that you will find that many alters do not like or trust you. You have to keep in mind the horror that the alters have experienced. Their job in the past was to keep your loved one as safe as possible, and to keep them alive at all costs. It was not their job to trust people, and to them, you are no different. It is possible to get alters to trust you, but it will take time.

Maybe you should start by simply

thanking them for everything they do

and have done for your loved one.

This could go a long way because I

have realized that a lot of alters hold

a lot of guilt. They may think they

should have been able to do more to

stop the abuse that was happening.

By you saying thank you it might help

them to see that they did all they

could do and that you are grateful to

them.

- You can be especially sensitive to child alters. Your loved one will act like a child when a child alter is out. These alters are very much the same as a real child, just in an adult body. Talk quietly to them and do not make sudden moves. They usually will scare extremely easily. You could offer to do things that a normal child would like. Coloring, putting together a puzzle, watching a movie, playing video games, or even eating candy are some things that a child alter might like to do. Child alters often do not get a lot of time out, so if possible, you should try to make this a very fun time for them. Remember that these little alters have seen and experienced things that no one should ever have to see or experience. They know a whole lot about the bad things in life, but very little about the good things. If a little one seems scared, you may be able to hold them, or give them a hug, if that would be appropriate. Do this with caution because these little ones

might view any kind of touch as bad.

When you spend time with little

ones, keep in mind that they are very

wounded by the past. They might not

always show it, but it is always there.

They need healing just as much as the

rest. A little one is not just going to

talk about the past and the hurt. They

do not know how and probably do

not know the right words. However,

if you listen careful while you are

spending time with them they might

say little things that you can build a

conversation on. Another thing to

remember about little ones is that

the whole system is probably very

protective of them. Even the angry

alters probably help look after them.

You want to make sure that you do

not do anything to hurt them. Never

lie to them or hurt them. If you make

a mistake with them work hard and

fast to correct it. If you do not, the

other alters might not let you have

any more contact with them, and

that would make it very hard to help your loved one. All of the alters need to heal, including the little ones, in order for everyone to truly be free from the past and learn to work together.

- You can remind your loved one, or an alter, of where they are and what they are doing , if you notice that they are having a flashback. Have them look around and tell you what they see. This will help ground them and remind them that the abuse is

not happening right now and that

what they are experiencing is just a

really strong memory. Maybe you can

get them to tell you about the

flashback, as I have found that this

helps to lessen the flashbacks over

time. At times, you may witness your

loved one in what seems to be very

real physical pain. Flashbacks can also

be felt physically. They can bring back

memories of abuse and your loved

one can feel the pain that they felt

then. Now of course this is only in the
mind but I am here to tell you that if
you are the one feeling it, you do not
not care if it is just in the mind. It
hurts just as it would if it were
happening all over again. This pain
can be stopped. Most times, just by
grounding and realizing that the
abuse happened a long time ago.
Talking about what they are feeling
will help as well. For the most part
grounding and talking will always
help. But you might be asking

140

yourself, "what happens when a child alter experiences these flashbacks". Child alters, while usually very intelligent, are not capable of adult reasoning. They, sometimes, are not aware that the body they live in has grown up. Even if they do realize the time that has passed, they may still be afraid that the abusers will come back. Or in there mind the events of the past might play repeatedly so often that they feel stuck in that time. Whatever the case may be,

watching a child alter have a
flashback, especially one where they
feel pain, can be horrible. When you
spend time with child alters you
really see just how "child like" they
are, and to see any child hurt and
terrified is difficult. Especially when it
seems that there is nothing you can
do. It may be hard, if not impossible,
to get a little one to realize that the
flashback is just a memory at the
time they are experiencing it. My
suggestions is to hold them, if it is

appropriate, and they will let you. Keep telling them in a quiet, calming voice that everything is going to be OK. Remind them that they are safe. If they say something hurts do whatever you would do if it were a real hurt. Sometimes this will help and sometimes it won't. Flashbacks are never fun or easy, but as your loved one works through, and heal from, the past, eventually they will decrease in severity and frequency.

- You can help your loved one by talking with them about what is going on. One of the main ways for your loved one to manage life with DID is learning to communicate with everyone on the inside. Communication is key because all these alters are sharing one body and are out at different times. Communication allows everyone to work together. It also cuts down on the fighting and disagreements amongst the alters. Maybe you can

offer suggestions when a
compromise needs to be made. For
example, two alters are fighting for
time out maybe you could help your
loved one figure out times when each
of them could have their own time
out.

- You can make sure to take care of
yourself, even while watching your
loved one go through this ordeal. In
order for you to help your loved one,
you also need to take care of

yourself. It is hard to watch anyone that you love go through difficult times. Not only will you see your loved ones go through difficult times but you will often see all the ones inside go through it as well. You may become the person that these alters begin to trust and feel safe enough to share the secrets they hold of the past. These secrets can be stories of horrific torture, abuse, and neglect. And at some point it will likely hit you that all of his happened to someone that you love very much. That can be very painful in itself. Make sure that you take time for yourself to deal with your own emotions as you help your loved on through all this through all this.

- We have talked about things you can do to help; now I want to talk about things not to do. First, never say that you understand what they are going through. There is no possible way that you could understand unless you have DID. Second, never belittle or make fun of how your loved one or one of their alters act. They cannot help it. Third, never compare them to anything that you have seen on TV. We all know that the media only wants to make money not give honest facts. Fourth, never think that you can treat all alters the same way. They are very separate and need to be treated as such. Fifth, never intentionally hurt or lie to an alter. This will break their trust and you

may never get it back. Sixth, never
tell them that it must be great to
have DID or that it must be great to
be able to hide when things get
tough, and have someone else take
over. This could not be farther from
the truth. There are not too many
people who would want to have DID.
Remember if someone has DID then
that means that they have
experienced some awful things in
their life.

- Supporting a loved one who has DID can be very tough at times, but also well worth it. You could be the only person that your loved one has ever let inside their world. That is trust like no other. Many people would be afraid to get to know someone with DID, but people with DID are actually quite amazing people. They are often very intelligent, but they do not believe that they are. They usually make very good friends because they know what it is like to be hurt and try very hard not to hurt anyone. If you are lucky enough to be a person that your loved one trusts, I promise that you will find it rewarding if you stick with it. Good luck and feel free to ask me any questions that you might have. You can ask them through my website

www.survivingchildhoodabuse.com.

Printed in Great Britain
by Amazon